Maintenance Your Marriage

A Proactive Guide To Building a Solid
Foundation In Your Marriage

Bettina Roseman

KAJ Legacy Press, LLC

For information on booking a speaking engagement with the author please forward requests to: marriagemaintenance@yahoo.com
10 9 8 7 6 5 4 3 2 1
Library of Congress Catalog Number: 2016936025
ISBN: 978-0-9973883-0-5
ISBN: 978-0-9973883-1-2 (Ebook)
Printed in the United States of America
Cover photo Credit - www.123rf.com

Dedication

This book is dedicated to the three loves of my life - Kiara, Amber, and Jacolby. You give me the strength to fight for every tomorrow God grants me to see.

Contents

Something to think about

Introduction

The idea behind being proactive in your marriage

> *I was living life as if certain things would never happen to me.*

● ● ●

I don't know why it took me going through the tragedy of a divorce in order to figure out how to be married, but it did. It's funny how we spend our lives believing that good things happen to good people. However, life has its way of producing an entirely different reality. Simply put, waking up with the best intentions and doing the right things will not always lead you to a happy ending. So just when I finally figured out this marriage thing I found myself sitting on my couch alone without my high school sweetheart and once soul mate. I am writing my heart away to get information to others to save them from this road that leaves gaping holes that are too painful to fill.

Let's first get one thing out in the open; I am in no way an expert on marriage (or relationships for that matter). I am not a therapist nor have I been to any higher institution of learning for psychology or any related field that could certify me as such an expert. With that being said, who am I and what in the world qualifies me to write a book on anything dealing with marriage? First, I would not be writing one word of this for you to read had it not been for my lovely sorority sisters who constantly encouraged me to write my experiences in a book. Now back to the question at hand, what qualifies me to write a book in order to tell you how to maintenance your marriage? I am bold enough to say that I am a woman who thought she had it all figured out, and I was living life as if certain things would never happen to me. I am bold enough to say that I thought certain things would naturally happen as a result of "living right" and focusing on my family. I am now wise enough to know that I was ignorant to so many things. I am a woman of God that has taken life's storms and used them to reflect and grow. My friends have told me that I have an old soul, but it is through my life experiences that I have gotten to this point.

Now that we have gotten that out of the way, I want to share one of the biggest revelations that came to me during my divorce, let's call this my "aha" moment. I remember sitting in my room and this question came to me as quickly as lightning strikes, "What in the hell did I do to maintenance my marriage?" My second thought was "Why in the hell am I just now thinking about this?" As I looked closely at the dictionary's definition of the word maintenance, I stumbled upon one version that read: *The work of keeping something in proper working condition; upkeep.*

> *Maintenance: The work of keeping something in proper working condition; upkeep.*

Perfect! Then I began to look at all of the things in my life that require some sort of maintenance, and the list was quite extensive. Every three months or five thousand miles I take my car in for an oil change to keep my engine from failing. During the change in seasons, I make sure to get my tire pressure checked to protect me from a blowout. Each year I make a doctor's appointment for a wellness check just to make sure things are looking as they should. Every year I go see my eye doctor to make sure that all systems are a go, and I visit my dentist to get my teeth cleaned and x-rayed. The more I thought about the aforementioned list and my mindset regarding each item, one thing became evidently clear - everyone of them was a non-negotiable and had to be done.

Since I am not a mechanic, doctor, or a dentist I had to trust an expert to provide those services for me. I often asked family and friends for a referral for the particular service that I needed so that I was in somewhat trusted hands. What came next was a series of events that showed my commitment to my maintenance plan. I took off of work or at least adjusted my schedule to make sure these things happened. In the end, it was worth following-through with each appointment because the alternative was much worse. The disasters that I avoided with my maintenance plan included a locked up engine or costly car repair, an undesired health event, or an expensive dental procedure. Being that I am so proactive when it comes to my health and my car, how did I miss the mark with my marriage?

So what exactly was my mindset when it came to my marriage? What were we proactively doing to make sure that it was cared for to ensure its survival? Who were we getting to help us? After all I had never been a wife before and he had never been a husband before, so how were we making sure that we were doing the right things to keep our marriage healthy and functioning year after year? I can tell you now that we used the system most marriages use, the good old "well we are still together" system,

> **After all I had never been a wife before and he had never been a husband before.**

the one and only "hope" system and I can't leave out that wonderful "we are so in love" system. All of which led to my big fat failed marriage. This book serves as a guide for married couples or people considering taking the next step of marriage. I hope that it gives you tangible steps to being proactive in developing and securing a maintenance plan for your marriage.

Gut check

Chapter one

Is your mindset proactive or reactive

$$\Big[\ \textit{What is the clinking noise in your marriage?}\ \Big]$$

● ● ●

I am really big on analogies and you will see them throughout this book. One of the things I find hilarious is how angry men get when the women in their lives fail to maintain their vehicles. On the flip side, women get equally as angry when the men in their lives fail to do things that require maintenance around the house. It is not unusual that a call for help comes when we hear a clinking sound or maybe when something in our car is driving differently, worst case the car won't even start. The influx of questions that come from the men in our lives are so specific; did you change the oil, have you put water in your battery, or how long has that indicator light been on? Women usually have a response of "I don't know" and "what is that going to help now," and "can you fix my car or take it to someone to get it fixed?" After paying sometimes hundreds or thousands of dollars to repair our vehicle, men sometimes cannot move from the fact that if we would have just mentioned the indicator light earlier none of this would be happening. In this likely scenario men are 100% on board with the maintenance plan and they find value in it, but women just want a running car.

Now let's flip the script to the almighty honey-do-list as it relates to the things that need to be done at home. The list includes things such as mowing the yard, taking out the trash, and even changing the filters in the AC unit. Ladies we have all experienced the day when we came home from work only to find that the trash had not been taken out and the trash man had already come. It is enough to make a woman go into hysterics. Women probe and probe to find out what got in the way of taking the trash out, while men secretly think, "No big deal, I'll take it out next time. Get off my back already." In this scenario women are 100% on board with the maintenance plan and they find value in it, and men just want them to stop nagging about the damn trash.

So let's compare this to our marriages. What is the clinking noise in your marriage? What is the something that isn't functioning quite right at the moment? Is your marriage at a complete stop with no start in sight? Who believes in the maintenance process and who doesn't? Is there something that could have been done before it got to this point? On the next pages you will see a Life Maintenance Checklist and a Marriage Maintenance Checklist for you and your spouse to complete separately. If you are single, just complete it on

> *What is the something that isn't functioning quite right at the moment?*

your own. I want you to give yourself points based on the table on page 10 for items that pertain to only you.

Use the table below to complete the following:

Life Maintenance Checklist: *Spouse A page 11-13*

                                       Spouse B page 17-19

Marriage Maintenance Checklist: *Spouse A page 14-15*

                                       Spouse B page 20-21

Points	Frequency
2	Always or Regularly
1	Occasionally or Sometimes
0	Absolutely Never

Spouse A

Life Maintenance Checklist

Place a number in the boxes using the table on pg. 10.

<u>Car</u>

☐	Get your oil changed
☐	Get your tires rotated
☐	Get your tire pressure checked
☐	Keep your battery water level filled
☐	Get your car inspection completed yearly
☐	Get your car filters/belts checked

_____

☐ Section Total

Health

☐ Go to the Doctor for checkups yearly

☐ Go to the Dentist every six months

☐ Go to the eye doctor yearly

☐ Go to a chiropractor

☐ Take your children to get yearly checkups and physicals

☐ Section Total

<u>Home</u>

☐ Change the filter in your home AC unit every 3-6 months

☐ Mow your yard

☐ Water your yard

☐ Fertilize your grass

☐ Take the trash out

☐ Section Total

Spouse A

Marriage Maintenance Checklist

Actions

☐ Have been to pre-marital counseling

☐ Have been to marriage counseling

☐ Do you attend any type of marriage conferences at least once a year

☐ Have you made appointments on a calendar with your mate (planned date nights, not the spontaneous ones)

☐ Have you had couples nights out

☐ Have you and your spouse intentionally talked about issues in marriages that you may or may not be facing

☐ Do you have written yearly goals as a married couple

☐ Do you track your progress together towards your goals

☐ Do you read articles or books at least once a year to study about marriage

☐	Do you have a mentor who is married that you can call
☐	Does your mate have a mentor who is married that he or she can call

☐	Section Total

Spouse A

Thoughts

Please place a check mark next to the selection you feel best reflects your thought process.

- ☐ Open to marriage counseling
- ☐ Object to marriage counseling (do not like people in your business)

- ☐ Open to having a marriage mentor
- ☐ Object to having a marriage mentor

- ☐ Like setting goals
- ☐ Hate setting goals

- ☐ Open to missing events for your children for a night out with your spouse

- ☐ Would rather plan your schedule around your children's events in order to work in both

Spouse B

Life Maintenance Checklist

Place a number in the boxes using the table on pg. 10.

<u>**Car**</u>

☐	Get your oil changed
☐	Get your tires rotated
☐	Get your tire pressure checked
☐	Keep your battery water level filled
☐	Get your car inspection completed yearly
☐	Get your car filters/belts checked

☐ Section Total

Health

☐ Go to the Doctor for checkups yearly

☐ Go to the Dentist every six months

☐ Go to the eye doctor yearly

☐ Go to a chiropractor

☐ Take your children to get yearly checkups and physicals

☐ Section Total

<u>Home</u>

☐	Change the filter in your home AC unit every 3-6 months
☐	Mow your yard
☐	Water your yard
☐	Fertilize your grass
☐	Take the trash out

☐	Section Total

Spouse B

Marriage Maintenance Checklist

Actions

☐ Have been to pre-marital counseling

☐ Have been to marriage counseling

☐ Do you attend any type of marriage conferences at least once a year

☐ Have you made appointments on a calendar with your mate (planned date nights, not the spontaneous ones)

☐ Have you had couples nights out

☐ Have you and your spouse intentionally talked about issues in marriages that you may or may not be facing

☐ Do you have written yearly goals as a married couple

☐ Do you track your progress together towards your goals

☐ Do you read articles or books at least once a year to study about marriage

☐	Do you have a mentor who is married that you can call
☐	Does your mate have a mentor who is married that he or she can call

☐	Section Total

Spouse B

<u>Thoughts</u>

Please place a check mark next to the selection you feel best reflects your thought process.

- ☐ Open to marriage counseling
- ☐ Object to marriage counseling (do not like people in your business)

- ☐ Open to having a marriage mentor
- ☐ Object to having a marriage mentor

- ☐ Like setting goals
- ☐ Hate setting goals

- ☐ Open to missing events for your children for a night out with your spouse

- ☐ Would rather plan your schedule around your children's events in order to work in both

Let's look at how you both did. Look at the life maintenance list first and compare your checklist to your spouse's? Are you surprised by any of the results?

Car	Description	Your Score	Spouse's Score
9-12	Car maintenance is critical		
5-8	Car maintenance is somewhat important		
0-4	Car maintenance is not a focus for you		

Home	Description	Your Score	Spouse's Score
8-10	Home maintenance is a must		
4-7	Home maintenance is somewhat important		
0-3	Home maintenance is not at the top of your list		

Health	Description	Your Score	Spouse's Score
8-10	Health maintenance is a must		
4-7	Health maintenance is somewhat a focus		
0-3	Health maintenance is not a focus at this time for you		

Maintenance Your Marriage

Now look at the Marriage Maintenance list and compare your checklist to your spouse's?

Marriage	Description	Your Score	Spouse's Score
19-22	Your Marriage and its maintenance is top priority and you have minimal vulnerable areas		
16-18	Your Marriage is vulnerable in very specific areas but marriage maintenance is important to you		
11-15	Your Marriage is vulnerable with a heavier focus in some areas and no focus in others		
6-10	Your Marriage is very vulnerable with a slight focus in 1-2 areas		
0-5	Your Marriage is extremely vulnerable in most areas		

The last section of your exercise digs deep into each of your thought processes and helps you to identify what each of you are open to and what you are not. Take a moment and compare your section titled Thoughts on pages 16 and 22 to your spouse's. Now don't panic and think that you are not meant to be with one another, it is just information for now. So relax, you are taking the best steps by reading this book. You will see shifts in certain areas of your thinking by the end of this book. Although you may find yourself hesitant of other ideas presented, remain open to try new things for the good of your marriage. Either way, you just did a huge piece of the work!   Knowing where each of you stands on these items is critical in knowing and respecting your individual views, thus helping you find your true starting point.

> *Remember the more that you both discover about one another up front regarding these issues equips you both to place yourself strategically in a proactive state.*

Some things may require a discussion and that is where you begin to build a maintenance plan for your marriage. Remember, the more that you both discover about one another up front regarding these issues equips you both to place yourself strategically in a proactive state.

Now we will take a look at some very specific areas to include in your maintenance plan ensuring you both are doing the work required so that "until death do us part" and not "we grew apart" is your reality. Let's do this work.

Standing your ground

Chapter two

Counseling is a non-negotiable

> *If you would have asked me prior to this how many times I had gone to counseling the answer would have been once, pre-marital counseling.*

● ● ●

Growing up, one of my favorite cartoons in the world was the Coyote and Road Runner (yeah that's old). I mean I would watch that cartoon day in and day out waiting on the day that the Coyote finally would catch the Road Runner. Day after day and week after week I watched but it just never happened, but for some reason I kept watching as if it were going to change. I must say that I felt like the Coyote at the end of my marriage, chasing something that at the end of each day evaded my grasp. Now the Coyote would set all types of traps in hopes that he would catch the Road Runner and every time those traps ended up back firing and hurting him. That is exactly what my reactive attitude to save my marriage did to me.

It is crazy, you should have seen me rounding up counselors from an outside agency, going to a pastor at my church, and I even went to group and individual counseling. If you would have asked me prior to this how many times I had gone to counseling during the 18 years of my relationship the answer would have been once, pre-marital counseling.

But things were different now, there was a fight that had to result in a win so I needed a mighty team, no an army of experts to save us. Taking it a step further, I was reading all of the books and articles in the world trying to overload myself with information so that I could save the marriage that was falling apart right before my eyes. I was trying to fix that which was so severely broken because my mindset and my previous expectations were all wrong. Why in the world did I not have a maintenance plan involving yearly counseling on my "must have" list before I said yes to his proposal? More importantly, why in the world did I not communicate that expectation to him at the time of his proposal as a deal breaker? It would have saved both of us lots of money on a wedding and divorce.

You know among my sorority sisters and other friends, (most of whom are married) we often get together and use one another as outlets. We often provide support by listening to the good the bad and the ugly, and we offer advice when it is needed.

One of the most frustrating things I have found when we discuss issues that each of us face in our relationships, is the view on attending marital counseling. Most of them have shared with me that their mates are not even willing to see a counselor no matter how big or small the problem is. I have some friends who have shared that their mates would let the marriage end

> *Most of them have shared with me that their mates are not even willing to see a counselor no matter how big or small the problem is.*

rather than go to someone who is going to be all up in their business. So I posed this question to my friends, "did you set an early expectation that counseling is just part of the deal?" All of them of course said no and went on to explain that they never thought about it like that. I mean, it was an afterthought for me as well, so I am not judging them. I am just frustrated at the state of their marriages and the one sided refusal to get help. No matter what stage your marriage is in you must involve a counselor.

The great news for you is that you are being proactive in developing a maintenance plan that involves yearly counseling. By doing so, my example to save a marriage is not your reality. So what does this look like and why in the world would a couple go to counseling every year? What if there is nothing wrong? My response to that is simple, when you go to the doctor every year you may not have any major health issues at that time, but you still want to make sure that everything below the surface is running on all cylinders. I really think counseling gets a bad rap, we go in and they tell us what is wrong and then they try to fix us and we don't want to be fixed because we are set in our ways.

Throw that mentality right out the door. Look at your mate now and tell them in order for us to continue to run on all cylinders we must go to counseling every year on the day we committed our lives to one another. What if you changed your mindset and viewed counseling simply as a tool used to ensure things are going exactly as planned? Things do not have to be going bad in order to see a counselor. It is a yearly investment by the two of you that says we need to go in for our checkup. When you go to counseling with this mindset you can freely discuss the little things, what's going well, where do we want to be in our marriage and what are the typical difficulties that married couples face? I want to give you a list of focus items for you and

> *What if you changed your mindset and viewed counseling simply as a tool that you use to ensure that things are going exactly where you both want them to be going?*

your spouse to consider when you begin this new journey. I want you to intentionally set this appointment on the day that you were married and worry about the date night and celebration after that visit. Your anniversary should be a celebration of the year ahead of you and not a relief that you made it through what's behind you.

Maintenance Your Marriage

What if things are going well for me and my spouse? What should we discuss?

- ☐ Financial goals (do you have a financial goal that you want to achieve but you both need to get on the same page with finances)

- ☐ Traveling goals

- ☐ Communicating effectively

- ☐ How to blend or involve our family

- ☐ Things are going well, what can we do to keep them that way

- ☐ Ask the counselor for typical marriage problems and how to safeguard your marriage

- ☐ How to date one another like you did before you were married

- ☐ Trying to find a balance between being a wife or husband, mother or father, and a professional and still maintain some of your independence

- ☐ Protecting your marriage against adultery

- ☐ Do a check in front of the counselor and ask your mate if you are meeting his/her needs

- ☐ Set a relationship goal, this year we will...by

- ☐ Set a family goal, this year we will....by

- ☐ Set an individual goal, this year I will.....how does your individual goal impact your home, and communicate what you need from your mate in order for that goal to happen.

☐ Tell one another what you have enjoyed to this point about one another

☐ Anything temporary/long term that will change in your home that effects the marriage (parent moving in, child returning home, child going to college, new baby, loss of job, extra job, promotion, going back to school, etc.)

☐ New insecurities (making your mate aware of what's going on inside of you)

> *You both begin to see counseling as a helpful tool without the one sided rejection to the counseling process.*

Can you visualize the problems or situations that you will get ahead of and even eliminate by talking about these things on a yearly basis? I wish someone would have told me these things 18 years ago. My life would have changed dramatically. Making this a yearly routine prepares your marriage to rely on this tool even when serious problems surface. You both begin to see counseling as a helpful tool without the one sided rejection to the counseling process. Think of the relationship you will establish with your counselor as each year passes, it almost mimics that of your primary care physician. Why is something so simple so far from the minds of most? I am excited for you and your spouse as you begin by choosing a counselor to begin this work. Marriage is some of the hardest work that you will ever do, and if you both can agree that you need the maintenance the hard part is over. If you are single, I encourage you to make counseling a part of your package. If he or she does not want to maintenance your marriage every single year with a counselor then he or she is not the one. It is a deal breaker and it is non-negotiable.

Priorities

Chapter three

Setting appointments with your mate

> $\Big[$*...when people make appointments they more often than not honor those appointments.*$\Big]$

● ● ●

I know it sounds weird to schedule appointments with your mate, but the rationale is simple, when people make appointments they more often than not honor those appointments. Even if someone cancels their appointments, some form of communication is there and usually people immediately reschedule. Let's use a doctor visit this time, you schedule an appointment for your annual check-up and you either put the date and time in your phone or on your calendar or maybe you carry around one of those appointment cards from your doctor's office. By making the appointment you move from "I need to go to the doctor" to "I am going to the doctor on a specific date" and you begin to reorganize the other areas in your life around that appointment.

Ladies, now I can just imagine that you are slightly turning your nose up at this idea because it does not leave room for spontaneity, which we so desperately desire. Let me assure you that for every scheduled appointment that I have made with my doctor, there has been the occasional walk-in appointment needed at an urgent care facility as well. You can still have the element of get up and go in your marriage, you just cannot use that as the basis for your entire relationship.

As I take a look back over my life I can tell you that I scheduled every appointment in the world and never once considered scheduling appointments with my now ex-husband. What is that old saying, if I only knew then what I know now? So it is no surprise that I created a habit of scheduling my marriage around every other appointment that I had set in my life. My marriage became the flexible piece and everything else in my life had priority over it. I would never intentionally do that and I can't tell you that he even noticed that it was being done. I mean seriously, can you even imagine doing that day in and day out and

> *My marriage became the flexible piece and everything else in my life had priority over it.*

confidently believing that your marriage was the priority in your life only to find out that it wasn't?

I remember at one of our counseling sessions towards the end of our marriage, the counselor told us to put up a calendar that the entire family could see. On this calendar we were supposed to set appointments (date night if you will) that were hard dates and we had to agree to stick to these dates even if our children had an event. The idea is that you intentionally set appointments for your marriage to be the priority throughout the year. Now you both can agree on the number of appointments that you set, it could be one or two a month, but the idea is that you set them regularly. I must admit I was a little skeptical to the idea of the calendar because we had unconsciously made the children the center of our marriage. Furthermore, we gave them complete priority over everything.

My first question to our counselor was what if the kids end up having a basketball game or something and we don't honor the date on the calendar? Our counselors response was shocking, because of course in my analytical mind I had just thrown her a curve ball or an exception to the calendar idea. She told us to sit our children down and show them the dates that we had on the calendar. She wanted us to explain to them that these are the dates that mommy and daddy need this month to make sure that we take care of our marriage. She said to teach them that if we didn't nurture our marriage that we would be putting our family at risk. She told us flat out that we were teaching our children to continue a cycle that we set, that the children at all cost come first. Up to this point I was skittishly taking in what she was saying until that last statement. That hit me like a ton of bricks. How could I possibly be teaching my children such a skewed reality?

She said to point out and acknowledge conflicts in scheduling that will arise, but the appointment that will be honored is the one that we had with one another. Her advice was for us to get someone to tape the event we were going to miss and watch it as a family on a later date. Wow! Prior to this exercise our dates on the calendar consisted of a gymnasium, a choir concert, or a Special Olympics event. We had become numb to the reality that we needed some "us" time on that calendar that didn't center on the kids. Now don't get me wrong, I don't want you thinking that my marriage was flat or that we did not date at all. We were actually best friends and again I will use the word soul mates, but we only went out occasionally without our children.

Have you ever heard the phrase *gross misconduct*? Well at the end of the day we were both guilty of *gross misconduct* in our marriage. It is so funny because I would sit around with my sorority sisters and say "girl this marriage thing does not come with a handbook". I had made something difficult

> *...we were both guilty of gross misconduct in our marriage...*

virtually impossible because I was trying to do it on my own and in my own way. To top it all off I was talking to women who were doing the very same thing to some degree and it validated that my struggle was real. I was so busy walking around with the "S" on my chest trying to make it all happen, and in doing that I lost everything. Looking back there were a wealth of resources and people that we could have invited into our marriage to make it work. The guess and check method did not work out for us. The great thing about this concept is no matter where you are in your marriage you can begin now to shift you and your spouse's mind set.

So here it goes, how do you start? Ask your spouse if you can schedule some time with him or her and put it on your calendar. Next, you both need to sit and agree that work, children, and other life events cannot interfere with these dates. Let me stress here that a one sided commitment will not work; you both have to agree whole heartedly that your marriage is the priority. You cannot view your job as more important than your spouse's job, thus giving yourself an exception to the calendar appointment non-cancellation policy. If you need to have a family meeting to go over this new practice with your children, then schedule that time. Remember the idea is to let your children know that in order for the family to function you have to nurture your marriage; the marriage has to come first. I am excited for you and your spouse as you intentionally schedule time with one another proving your commitment to prioritizing your marriage.

Team up

Chapter four

Finding a Marriage Mentor

> *I can remember the ideology behind mentors and mentorship from a very young age.*

● ● ●

I can remember the ideology behind mentors and mentorship from a very young age. Many of my memories derive from being in after school care and having Big Brothers and Big Sisters programs through the Boys and Girls Club that I attended. Over the past year, I really began to explore the mentor and mentorship relationship through an adult lens. I found myself looking at all of the professions that require some type of mentorship program to be completed prior to being hired or becoming certified to even enter the profession. In the medical field students are required to go through a residency program with accomplished doctors as their mentors. The law enforcement field pairs rookie cops with veteran officers who serve as mentors for a given period of time. Even in the world of religion, preachers have mentor pastors as they begin the journey of starting their own ministry.

As an educator during my first year on the job, I was assigned a mentor by the name of Mrs. Walker. I had a principal who evaluated my job performance, a content leader who ensured that I was teaching what the state of Texas required, but Mrs. Walker made sure that I was okay day in and day out. She was someone I could share my real struggles with without the fear of some sort of negative implication. Once she listened she would give me her unbiased thoughts of what was going on, give me advice and motivate me to get back in there and try again. She would identify where I was wrong or where I was right and even tell me where and how I could use certain experiences to grow. Sometimes she would just listen and that was enough. I cannot stress to you how valuable that relationship was for me. I could not wait to get to a point in my career where I could return the favor to another educator. To this day, I have a mentor that I go to regularly to help me in my professional world. The fact that this is such a critical piece in my professional life leaves me wondering why in the hell I had not adopted this in my marriage. Now don't get me wrong, I have great girlfriends that I can talk to, but I have never had a marriage mentor. In order to be a mentor, you at some point had to have walked in the shoes that I am currently wearing. So if your friend is unmarried or got married at the same time that you did, he or she is not mentor material.

> *Find a person that embodies the things that are important to you.*

Eighteen years in a state that I had never experienced before (since it was my first marriage) and no one on my team helping to guide me on the path before me resulted in disaster. Now remember I said that I was scraping and fighting to save my marriage towards the end, well I went to a minister at my church for weekly counseling and he asked if I had a mentor. He then asked if my now ex-husband had a mentor. The answer was no. At that point I found a mentor like person (married less time than me but a great friend) and my ex kept repeating the fact that he did not talk to people like that (so he never found one). I will say this is the hardest piece for some people, and I would encourage you to truly soul search to find a person who has been married at least 10 years or more. If you are already married find someone who has been married five to ten years longer than you. Find a person that embodies the things that are important to you; so if you are grounded spiritually or if you have children then find someone who shares those experiences. Even if you begin seeing a counselor yearly, you will need a mentor to be there during the other three hundred and sixty four days.

One of the things that I found myself screaming to my then husband as we were fighting to save our marriage was, "you only consult yourself so how do you know that you are right...go ask somebody and come back and tell me what they said." When you only acknowledge things through your lens you are wrong. Marriage is such an intricate thing and not consulting with someone is almost as deadly as refusing to consult with a medical professional on things associated with our overall health. Now herein lies the problem, where do I find this mentor? Before we answer that question you must remember one important thing, the mentor relationship cannot be for one spouse and not the other. If you are having a hard time finding a mentor then begin a couples night so that you can meet couples and find a mentor, consult your church pastor and let them know you are looking for someone, or ask your counselor for help.

> *"...when choosing a mentor make sure you do not pick anyone who is #teamyou and at all cost will see things your way..."*

Another important consideration when choosing a mentor is making sure you do not pick anyone who is #teamyou and at all costs will see things your way. I call these people your cosigners. The right mentor will hold you accountable for your part in your marriage and guide you through the rest. This person will help you to honor your commitment to your appointments with your spouse and attending your yearly counseling sessions. This person will listen to the good, the bad, and the ugly and find the best solution even if it is not what you thought. When this person offers different advice than what you expected you listen because you trust their experience in marriage. I would seriously advise you and your spouse to find a mentor and introduce one another to the mentor that you have each chosen, but keep the relationship separate. You do not want to share the same mentor; men should have a male mentor and women should have a female mentor - no exceptions.

I am so excited for you and your spouse as you add this piece to your maintenance plan for your marriage. Be patient with one another as you seek to find the ideal mentor for yourselves. Don't let discouragement keep you from looking and don't give up; your marriage is worth the fight.

Avoiding disaster

Chapter five

Develop an emergency plan

[*What would you do in case of an emergency in your marriage?*]

● ● ●

Now it's time to develop an emergency plan for your marriage. Ok, now I know many of you are saying, "I have been with you up until this point." Hear me out. Have you thought about it, what would you do in case of an emergency in your marriage? Our homes are beautiful and we have insurance to cover them, but what if a fire broke out and burned your house down? Where are you going to sleep? Even with our vehicles, we pay monthly insurance, but one accident could total our car leaving us stranded. We know that we would drive a rental while we wait on the parties involved to restore us to our original state. Just as these situations require an emergency plan, we need to discuss the not so desirable things that can occur in your marriage to develop a solid plan. For the record, my emergency plan was the equivalent of attempting to buy fire insurance after the fire has already destroyed everything.

Now that we have identified the need, let's take a look at the details. What areas in your marriage could benefit from you and your spouse having an emergency plan in place? One thing to stress here is anything can become an emergency, and I am in no way suggesting that you take each possible event in your life and create an emergency plan. What I am suggesting is that you look at some big picture things and use those to develop a plan.

The following are a few suggestions to get you on the right track in order to put an emergency plan in place. This portion can be tied into the counseling sessions in Chapter 2.

What will you do:

❖ In case of a Financial Crisis in the marriage?

We all know how funny money can be to us in life. It is the one thing that determines the level of independence that we have in order to care for ourselves. Since you know that without it or without someone who has it, you would have some serious issues, you really need to think about what you will do if a major financial event occurs. First sit down and define what is considered a financial crisis for your marriage? We all know that a crisis to one person is not necessarily a crisis to another person. Is it the loss of an income or the addition of an unexpected expense, like kids going to college or purchasing a new car? Now that you have defined it, take a look at the impact and create a response. Who will get the extra job if needed? Are you willing to borrow money from loved ones until you get back on your feet? If you had to be displaced due to a financial crisis where would you live? When is it okay to dip into savings or retirement accounts? Again, I know that it is impossible to prepare for every financial crisis that you will experience in your married life. Please understand this is a surface level conversation that reduces the stress level in the event of a crisis because you both have done the work of trying to be on the same page up front. The number one thing that I heard while I was married was that money and communication were the top reasons that people got divorced. Remember a failure to plan is a plan to fail.

❖ In case of a major health event during the marriage?

I remember seeing a couple who within the first couple of months of their marriage were faced with a reality that had left one of them restricted to a wheel chair permanently. They had both literally walked down the aisle and danced away at their reception, but life had a different reality waiting for them just months later. No one could plan for this and as tragic as it seemed they are still married today and have a child that is so full of life. Have you ever considered what you would do if a major health event happened during your marriage? Do you really know what your spouse would do? Is this something that you want to hope that you are right about? The idea here is to communicate your beliefs about life support, DNR (do not resuscitate) orders, terminal illness, and even medical conditions that would require extended time off of work. I know it seems like a drag but again the idea is to just peek inside your spouse's mind and get an understanding of where they stand with regards to this. You have to remember that you were a whole person with a set of universal beliefs before you met your spouse. Making an assumption about a person's core beliefs would be one of the biggest mistakes that you could possibly make. Conversations that could develop around this include life insurance policies, maybe obtaining a type of catastrophic coverage in case a life event happens, or even money that can be used from an emergency fund that will only be touched if something happens. You both should also consider a line of credit or getting an emergency credit card that you can use. The hardest conversations to have are proven to have the greatest impact.

❖ In case of a major event with our parents or caregivers during the marriage?

Let's take a look at our parents or the people who acted as a caregiver to us in our youth. What happens when they grow older and can no longer live independently? You and your spouse have a certain mentality on what you will do when it comes to your parents/caregiver. My mind is made up that if my mom needs me then I am going to be there. She has just been so awesome in my life that without hesitation, I would do what would be required to help her. Can you imagine your spouse coming home with their parents by their side and then inform you that they will be living with you all? No matter the attempt to sympathize or understand you will have some level of resentment to the idea because of how it is being presented. I encourage you to have a conversation about your parents and remember it is a surface level conversation so you can gain an understanding of where your spouse's beliefs are. Potential focus areas could include nursing home options (or living in your home), financial support limits, or even transportation needs (once they can no longer drive).

Please do not think that if you all differ in this area that it means you are not meant for one another. Find the place of compromise and again take it to your counselor and work through it before it becomes your reality. Great news is discussing it when it is not a reality gives you more time to look at all the options without the pressure of time.

❖ In case of a major violation of the wedding vows by one or both parties?

Last but certainly not least, let's talk about violations of your vows. Why is this part of your emergency plan? I will tell you that if you do not secure those vows and the expectations around them more than on the day of your wedding, you are playing with fire with no fire extinguisher. Now I must say that on my wedding day I was so in tune with my vows, holding on to every word that I was asked to repeat as if they were the only words that had meaning in the world. The days and years after I said them, I never had a discussion about them with my now ex-husband. I went forward just making sure to honor my vows and assumed that he would do the same for the rest of our lives. What will you do if one of you breaks any of your vows? What is the plan of attack? Here are the typical vows that couples make to one another:

- Love and comfort one another

- Honor and keep one another for richer or poorer

- For better or worse

- In sickness and health

- Forsaking all others, be faithful only to him/her

- For as long as you both shall live

I really encourage you to first discuss the non-negotiable details of each one of these vows with one another. What does love and comfort mean to each one of you? What if there comes a time when you are not feeling loved or comforted? What is your plan then? Will you go see your counselor or will you develop a way to communicate your need to your spouse that is clear? What does forsaking all others specifically mean to each of you? Will personal communication be allowed with the opposite sex? Will friends of the opposite sex be allowed? What if someone violates this vow, what is your plan of action? Do you see when you really get into the details of the vows you are able to communicate your beliefs around them? It will be the small conversations that help to avoid the bigger violations of your vows. I would rather discuss with a counselor that my spouse violated the forsaking all others vow by having some type of communication that is not allowed rather than discussing a full blown affair. The idea here is easy; define the broad vows so you both know the specific expectations, then discuss what you will do if a violation occurs. Most importantly clearly define what things are non-negotiable. If there is a violation we automatically go to our counselor. This will also work if you and your spouse have written your own vows, just use the commitments included in them. I am excited for you and your spouse and the development of your emergency plan as you finalize the plan to maintenance your marriage.

You both can do this

Conclusion

Ready, set, let's go to work!

[*Your marriage is worth it!*]

● ● ●

You and your spouse are one mindset away from having the marriage of your dreams. We invest thousands upon thousands of dollars on the wedding leaving us to ponder what we are investing in the marriage on a daily, weekly, monthly, and yearly basis. It takes two to do this work, so a one-sided commitment is a commitment to fail. I am in no way suggesting that this and this alone will save you from every problem that you will have in your marriage. Nor am I providing some guarantee that huge problems and arguments will now be avoided. What I am pleading for you both to do is to be proactive and to commit to developing a plan to maintenance your marriage because forever is a very long time. Marriage is some of the hardest work that you will ever do and its rewards can be so fulfilling, but its heartache can last a lifetime. No one stands up in front of their loved ones and vow to love one another for now, that vow is until death.

The first step is to get on the same page with your beliefs as it pertains to your marriage. When you both began to read this book, you evaluated what you were open to. Take a look at your responses and discuss where you are now. Are you open to at least trying some of the ideas in this book? Do you see a shift in your mindset about the work behind putting together a maintenance plan for your marriage? Decide on a counselor and be open to the idea of a trusted team helping you and your spouse have the marriage of your dreams. Please don't be one of those couples who are so protective about their business that you lose the very marriage that you are keeping in secret. Start with this simple question; do we want a male or female counselor? It may take a couple of appointments to find the right fit but hang in there. Setting those appointments with one another in the next steps shows your spouse that your marriage is the priority. Identify and explain conflicts that will come about, but your marriage takes priority over everything else. Remember that this work will be rounded off by finding a mentor and developing those emergency plans for your marriage. You and your spouse should open Pandora's Box to many conversations that will give clarity to who each of you are below the surface. The great news for both of you is having this early discussion gives both of you time to develop healthy compromises and avoid the disasters that lead to divorce. So get ready, get set, and go do this work together. Your marriage is worth it!

Bettina Roseman

About the Author

Hi, I'm Bettina and I am a survivor of the pains and trials that divorce brings. I have been through some of the most difficult days that I have ever experienced in my 38 plus years of living. Over the past two years I have focused 100 percent of my attention on coming out on the other side of this point of pain in my life.

I believe that every marriage truly has a chance of lasting forever with the right tools in place. That belief along with my own life experiences inspired me to write this book. I am determined to help couples to see that when they shift their mindset about their marriages they are better equipped to face the forever that lies ahead of them. While marriage is some of the hardest work couples will do, it is also some of the most rewarding work when couples learn how to do it properly.

Interested in booking Bettina as a motivational speaker on Developing a Proactive Marriage Mindset please submit requests to: MarriageMaintenance@yahoo.com

*available for book signing and meet & greet

Acknowledgements

Where would I be without the amazing people who support my dream. My passion for the message in *Maintenance Your Marriage* has been welcomed by so many couples who truly want the happily ever after that they vowed to one another. Their realities have made this work simply put, better.

To the heart and soul of my project, my publishing family at KAJ Legacy Press, your work to make this project soar into greatness is nothing but a pure blessing. I also want to sincerely thank Michelle McKissic for pushing the timeline in editing this project. Dedra Shores, The Startup Stylist, your business wisdom is top notch. Having you to consult with throughout this process has made the impossible possible. Thank you for taking every bump along this path and turning it into an opportunity to learn and grow.

To my lovely line sisters of Delta Sigma Theta Sorority Incorporated, your belief in the author inside of me began a long time ago. Your support throughout this process has been my driving force. Thank you ladies!

I am truly better because of situations that were designed to break me. I never thought that I could lose everything and gain the world. To my loving family who I would be insane without, thank you for your support. I want to give a special thanks to my mom who is the definition of inspiration. To my wonderful children, Amber, Jacolby, and Kiara, you have been everything from my editor to my event planner on this project. You have been so supportive and it has truly meant the world to me. I can only hope that seeing me chase my dream will inspire you to live yours.

www.ingramcontent.com/pod-product-compliance
Lightning Source LLC
LaVergne TN
LVHW051202080426
835508LV00021B/2766